Donated in
memory of
Sylvester
Martin by his
loving family

1997

CEREBRAL PALSY

CEREBRAL PALSY

NATHAN AASENG

A VENTURE BOOK

FRANKLIN WATTS
NEW YORK • LONDON • TORONTO • SYDNEY

Library of Congress Cataloging-in-Publication Data

Aaseng, Nathan.
    Cerebral palsy / Nathan Aaseng.
        p.   cm. — (A Venture book)
    Includes bibliographical references and index.
    Summary: Discusses the causes, effects, prevention, and treatment of the debilitating condition known as cerebral palsy, which may occur in many different forms.
    ISBN 0-531-12529-7
    1. Cerebral palsy.   [1. Cerebral palsy.   2. Physically handicapped.]   I. Title.
RC388.A25   1991
616.8'36—dc20   91–18558 CIP AC

Contents

6

I am grateful for the assistance and cooperation so willingly provided by Ruth Gullerud, Joyce Weiss, Joey Brownell, Marilyn Anderson, Tom Dahl, and the staff at Putnam Heights School.

*Children with and without cerebral palsy
celebrating Halloween together*

1

What Is Cerebral Palsy?

Imagine that humans were rooted to the ground like trees, arms locked in one position like branches. Or suppose we floated limply in the water, able to travel only where the winds and currents carried us.

All that stands between us and such existence is our neuromuscular system. Many of us may not think much about muscle coordination except when we strike out at baseball or try to lift a heavy weight or learn tricks such as juggling. But muscles, working in coordination with impulses from the nerves, give us wonderful freedom of movement. They allow us to travel about, to seek what we want and need, to perform meaningful tasks, to communicate, and to entertain ourselves. The power and coordination provided by muscles and nerves allow us the independence to determine a great deal of our own destiny.

The human body, however, is not a perfect machine, and the fact that we are human does not mean we are automatically given this gift of neuromuscular control. An estimated three-quarters of a million people in the United States do not have the control that many of us take for granted, because they have *cerebral palsy*.

Defining Cerebral Palsy

For many reasons, cerebral palsy is difficult for the experts to describe. Some call it a disease because of its damaging effect on the body. Yet it is not like many diseases that are treatable or that continue to cause damage in the absence of treatment. Rather, it is something that happened once to the affected person and left its permanent mark. For this reason, cerebral palsy is more commonly referred to as a condition rather than a disease.

Cerebral palsy does not fit neatly into a definition because it affects people in so many different ways. People with cerebral palsy do not look alike, act alike, or sound alike any more than would a sample group of people in any population. Not only are there different types of cerebral palsy, but there are widely varying degrees of each of these types. One person with cerebral palsy may show no signs of it other than slightly slurred speech; another may be virtually unable to function. A host of related symptoms can accompany each type of cerebral palsy, from blindness to mental retardation. There is no simple way to describe the condition in a way that covers all the possible disorders or disabilities that may result. Nor can a simple definition include all its possible causes.

The term *cerebral palsy* offers only a general description of the problem. *Cerebral* is a word that refers to the brain, or more specifically, to the cerebrum—the two wrinkled masses that make up the largest part of the brain. *Palsy* can mean either paralysis (inability to move) or an uncontrolled tremor. The term *cerebral palsy* is meant to describe an abnormality of the brain

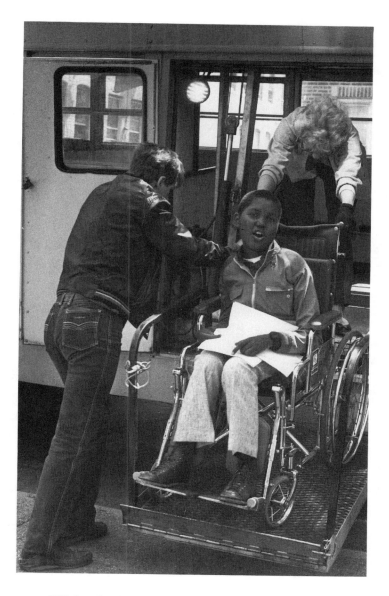

With a little help from modern technology,
people with CP can get out in the world.

that interferes with the normal function of the muscles.

Cerebral palsy is a *developmental* condition. It does not affect an organ such as the heart, which begins pumping blood well before birth and keeps performing the same function throughout one's life. It affects the neuromuscular system, and there is a world of difference between what a person can do with his or her muscles at age one and at age twenty-one. Cerebral palsy interferes with the ability to develop muscle control in a normal fashion. Strokes and brain injuries to fully developed adults are not considered cerebral palsy even though they may cause a similar muscle disability. Cerebral palsy is restricted to those brain abnormalities that occur before or at birth, or at any time in the first five years of life.

Finally, any definition of cerebral palsy must include the fact that it may involve disabilities other than muscle control. It is a multiply disabling condition that may affect a person's senses, intelligence, ability to learn, personality, and emotions.

There are no precise figures as to how many people are affected by cerebral palsy or exactly what progress is being made in the fight against it. Since cerebral palsy is not contagious and is not a threat to the general public, doctors have not been required to report cases to health boards. Because of the many related problems that may also occur with the condition, people with cerebral palsy are sometimes included in other categories of disabilities. The fact that cerebral palsy is not curable has made it a less attractive field of medical research in the past, and so relatively little research is done compared with that done on other health problems.

The best estimates of the United Cerebral Palsy Associations are that 750,000 Americans have one or more symptoms of cerebral palsy. This makes it the

Youngsters with CP enjoy watching sports...

...and playing sports.

most widespread lifetime disability in the nation. Roughly 5,000 new cases occur each year in the United States. The odds of a newborn developing cerebral palsy are somewhere between 1 to 1.5 infants per 1,000 live births.

The important things to remember about cerebral palsy are:

- It directly affects control of the muscles.
- This lack of control is caused by damage to the brain or lack of brain structures.
- This damage occurs before or at birth, or during the first five years of life.
- The condition can range from mild to severe.
- It may be accompanied by a number of other disabilities.

Cerebral palsy is *not*:

- A primary cause of death.
- A disease that gets worse with time.
- Contagious. It cannot be spread from one person to another.
- Curable. Those who have cerebral palsy will have it for their entire life.
- Inherited.

Cerebral Palsy in History

Although it was not recognized until the middle of the nineteenth century, cerebral palsy has certainly been around a long time. For as long as humans have had brains, there has been the possibility that something might go wrong with that organ. The earliest evidence of cerebral palsy symptoms that historians have uncovered appears in Mexican and Egyptian stone carv-

CP dates back as far as ancient Egypt.

ings dating back thousands of years. For most of history, however, cerebral palsy cases were simply lumped with other diseases and deformities that limited muscular movement.

It was not until 1843 that William Little, senior physician at London Hospital, detected a pattern in some of these conditions. In a series of published lectures, Little declared that a significant number of disabling conditions occur in babies born prematurely. Although he went a little too far in supposing that prematurity was the main factor in children's physical disabilities, he offered the valuable general observation that the fetus was "subject to diseases, particularly regarding deformities." Little used the term "spastic rigidity" in describing a state of constantly contracted muscles, a condition that he believed a child could develop before birth.

Delving more deeply into this unexplored subject, Little discovered that there was more to it than he had first supposed. In a lengthy study of more than two hundred cases of childhood disabilities, he began to develop a much clearer picture of what was causing these developmental problems. Moving away from his previous belief, Little declared that the main cause of these disabilities was asphyxiation, or lack of oxygen to the brain. A proper supply of oxygen, he concluded, could be threatened in the womb, or during labor and delivery.

In 1862, Little published a paper on the subject in order to spread the word to other physicians that abnormal deliveries could produce problems long after both mother and child recovered. Among the disabilities that he connected with difficult deliveries were "impairment of intellectual powers, epilepsy, temper, spastic rigidity, and loss of use of limbs." Showing a remarkable insight into the nature of this condition, Little pointed out that it was not always easy to distinguish physical handicaps from mental handicaps. In some cases, he concluded, retarded mental development "appears to result less from permanent injury to the brain than from the want of sufficient training and education."

Little performed such a valuable service in calling attention to the subject of infantile disabilities that the condition became known as Little's disease. This name was commonly used until the middle of the twentieth century. In Great Britain, the term "spastic," which Little coined, is still a synonym for cerebral palsy.

Near the end of the nineteenth century, Sigmund Freud published a book on Little's disease. Freud, who was better known for his pioneering work in psychology, gathered evidence that the childhood disabilities first described by Little could take many forms. Along with others, he referred to this general group of disabilities as "infantile cerebral paralysis." "Cerebral palsy" is a shortened form of that description.

Little's belief that some symptoms of infantile paralysis could be eased by proper training did not catch on right away. The more popular notion that nothing could be done to help such children stifled research in this area for many years. In the early 1900s, however, an intense interest in cerebral palsy arose at Children's Hospital in Boston, Massachusetts. There it was recognized that, while there was no one treatment for this condition, a combined effort among different specialists could treat many of its facets. At the same time, the new field of physical therapy was developing ways to improve coordination in persons previously thought to be beyond help.

Lingering doubts about the value of research for an incurable condition continued to hamper medical efforts at understanding cerebral palsy until the 1930s. Then, just as research was increasing, the world was plunged into a terrible war that consumed the time and resources of the medical world. Following the war, cerebral palsy benefitted from a spurt of interest in treating physical injuries to war veterans.

In the mid-1940s, more than a hundred years after William Little first described the condition, two organizations were formed that established cerebral palsy as an important area of medical study. In 1945, a small group of parents in New York formed the United Cerebral Palsy Association to promote education and research into the condition that was affecting their children. Two years later, a group of physicians focused professional attention on cerebral palsy by founding the American Academy for Cerebral Palsy.

The Many Forms of Cerebral Palsy

The many combinations of problems associated with cerebral palsy make it difficult to sort individuals with the condition into neat categories. There are dangers in putting a single label on people who display more differences than similarities with one another. Medical professionals, however, find it useful to categorize cerebral palsy types according to similar symptoms.

The most common classification of persons with cerebral palsy is by how the muscles are affected:

Spastic. Probably as many as two-thirds of all persons with cerebral palsy can be grouped in the category of spastic. Spastic cerebral palsy involves a constant state of *hypertonia*, unusual stiffness or tension in certain muscles. If you were to loosely clench your fist and leave it clenched all day, you would get a very rough idea of what it is like to be spastic. This muscle contraction is a reflex; that is, it happens without any conscious effort. This reflex is so strong that the person has difficulty making the muscle respond to his or her own wishes.

Athetoid. Roughly one-fourth of cerebral palsy conditions fall under the athetoid classification. While the muscles in spastic cerebral palsy are generally contracted in one position, the muscles in athetoid cerebral palsy are in constant motion. This motion, known as *dyskinesia*, may take the form of slow writhing and twisting, facial grimacing, or sudden jerks, all of which are reflex actions beyond the person's control. Stress and emotions can cause this unwanted activity to become even more noticeable.

Ataxic. Ataxic cerebral palsy is a less common form that primarily involves interruption of balance. Less than one out of ten cases of cerebral palsy result in the unsteadiness and lack of fine motor coordination that characterize ataxia.

These categories, however, are not edged with neat boundaries. Many people with cerebral palsy have combinations of these characteristics, the most common being spastic athetoid.

Another way of grouping cerebral palsy cases is by the area of the body affected. Since it is the arms and legs that provide the bulk of the motion for the human body, the divisions are made according to which limbs are most affected:

Hemiplegia. Hemiplegia means that one side of the body, including one arm and one leg, is impaired. More than a third of those with cerebral palsy are affected in this way.

Quadriplegia. Possibly 20 percent of cerebral palsy cases are quadriplegic. It is the most severe symptom of the condition, involving spastic or flaccid paralysis of all four limbs as well as the trunk.

Diplegia. Diplegia, also common in 20 percent of cerebral palsy cases, affects either both arms or both legs but involves the legs much more than the arms.

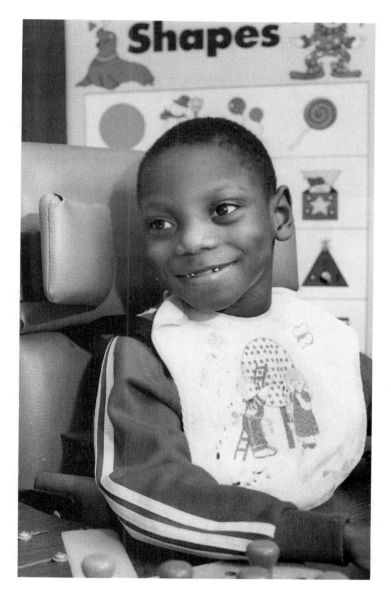

*Quadriplegia affects movement of the limbs but not
the ability to learn or smile.*

Paraplegia. Paraplegia is a form of paralysis that affects only the legs. It occurs in another 20 percent of the cerebral palsy population.

Monoplegia. Monoplegia involves paralysis of only one extremity or one muscle or a group of muscles and occurs rarely.

Classification by muscle types can be combined with the previously listed classifications to give a shorthand description of a cerebral palsy condition, for example, spastic hemiplegia, in which one arm and one leg on the same side of the body are often curled or contracted in ways that make normal movement difficult.

The United States Cerebral Palsy Athletic Association has divided cerebral palsy symptoms in a third way. In order to promote fair athletic competition among those with cerebral palsy, the association has created eight classes, based on how well the individual is able to perform certain muscular movements. Grouping by muscular ability can be useful in setting up facilities and therapy programs for the treatment of the condition.

Related Disabilities

Cerebral palsy can involve more than the random contraction or twitching of muscles, or difficulties in walking and the use of hands. The tongue is a muscle that may be affected by brain damage, and the inability to direct it affects the ability to form words. Some people with cerebral palsy may have great difficulty speaking, and others may be unable to make themselves understood at all. Lacking the ability to either speak or move, a person with a severe case of cerebral palsy may be isolated from human interaction, unable to communicate in any way.

The brain acts as the control tower, not only for

the activities of the muscles, but also for other systems of the body. Therefore, it is not surprising that when the brain is damaged severely enough to disrupt muscle coordination, systems other than the neuromuscular may also be impaired. Persons with cerebral palsy have a higher risk than the average population of developing one or more of the following in addition to their muscle control problems:

- impairment of the senses (blindness, deafness)
- convulsions or seizures
- mental retardation
- behavioral problems, such as hyperactivity
- emotional problems
- learning disabilities, such as attention deficit

The United Cerebral Palsy Associations estimate that a clear majority of those affected by cerebral palsy have three or more of the above disabilities. The fact that cerebral palsy can show up in such a variety of forms creates problems in studying the subject. Few statements about cerebral palsy will be true for all or even most people with the condition. Only by stepping back and taking in the vast range of challenges can the subject be kept in focus.

2

The Causes and Prevention of Cerebral Palsy

Dr. Little was on the right track when he suggested a link between premature birth and cerebral palsy. He was on another right track in concluding that a lack of oxygen in the brain was a major cause. Cerebral palsy cannot be traced to any single cause. The condition occurs as a result of damage to the brain. Because of the delicate nature of this organ, there are many ways in which such damage can take place.

The Vulnerable Brain

The human brain is made up of approximately 11 billion brain cells. The nerve cells of the brain are incapable of the rapid, complete healing that occurs in muscle cells. Rather, they are like expensive glassware—once damaged, there is virtually no way to make them as good as new.

Humans could not survive for long if this vital, vulnerable organ were not protected by the skull. This sturdy shield of bone can deflect most of the accidental bumps and blows that strike the head. But it is not

25

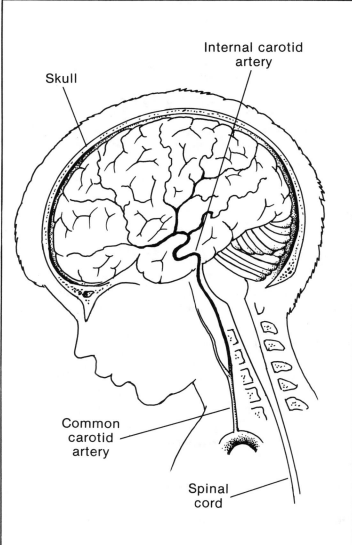

Skull

Internal carotid artery

Common carotid artery

Spinal cord

Cerebral palsy occurs as a result of damage to the brain received through head injury, disease, malnourishment, or other causes.

invincible. A very hard knock can break down the protective barrier and damage the brain. Serious brain injuries are far more likely to occur in very small children, whose skulls have developed insufficiently to offer adequate protection.

The skull is also of no use against damaging agents, such as infections, that penetrate through the body systems. As with accidents, the damage that results from such causes cannot be repaired.

The brain is also vulnerable because it depends on a constant supply of nourishment, particularly oxygen. It cannot slow down or shut down activity when the blood supply is low and then revive when the supply returns. If the flow of blood to the brain is interrupted for just a few minutes, serious and permanent damage can take place.

A long period of undernourishment can be just as serious as a short period of total blockage. If a person eats too little of the right foods, the body will be unable to supply nutrients to its vital organs. Again, small children are especially at risk of brain damage occurring from lack of nutrients to the brain. A constant supply of nutrients, particularly proteins, is especially vital while the brain is growing and developing at a very young age. Much of this development takes place before birth, in the mother's womb. Roughly 80 percent of a person's total number of brain cells are formed by age one and a half. By age four, when the average child weighs approximately 20 percent of adult weight, the brain has already reached 90 percent of its adult weight. If growth is interrupted or stopped during these early years, it can never be made up later in life.

The specific causes of cerebral palsy can be divided into three time periods in which they occur: during pregnancy (prenatal), during actual birth (perinatal), and in infancy.

Brain Damage Before Birth

The chemical blueprints that determine a person's characteristics are passed from parent to child through tiny bits of nucleoprotein known as genes. Some of the genetic instructions carried by these genes may be faulty. Defective genes are known to cause more than 200 types of birth defects. While cerebral palsy itself cannot be inherited, in a small minority of cases, genetic factors may lead to brain damage that results in a cerebral palsy. Defective genetic instructions may interfere with the chemical reactions that produce normal cell division and growth, or they may prevent an adequate supply of oxygen and other nutrients from reaching the brain.

One example of a harmful chemical reaction is the Rh blood factor. In rare cases, one parent may have red blood cells that are Rh positive while the other has cells that are Rh negative. When these two types of blood are mixed, anti-infection agents within one blood type attack the red blood cells of the other. A fetus may then inherit a blood type from the father that is incompatible with that of the mother. Since the mother's bloodstream supplies nutrients directly to the fetus, mixing of the two blood types is unavoidable in pregnancy. The mother's anti-infection agents, called antibodies, attack the red blood cells of her child. This Rh incompatibility does not affect the first pregnancy but may harm fetal red blood cells in pregnancies that follow.

While the fetus in the mother's womb is well sheltered from the outside world, illnesses that the mother contracts can be passed on to her child. Illnesses that may be nothing more than a minor nuisance to an adult may be serious enough to prevent proper brain development in the fetus.

One such disease is a contagious viral infection

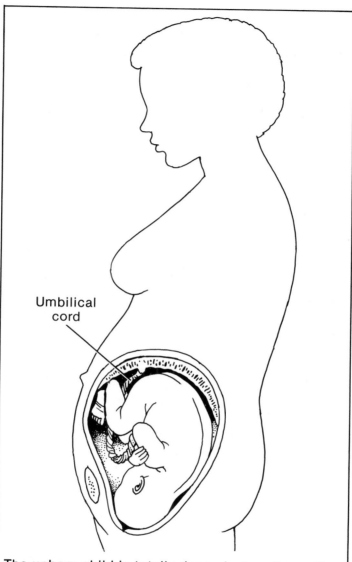

Umbilical
cord

The unborn child is totally dependent on its mother.
If the mother takes drugs or is sick or is in any
other way unhealthy, the child will receive the
"bad medicine" through the umbilical cord.

known as rubella, or German measles. This mild form of measles generally causes only mild discomfort in children and adults, but when contracted during pregnancy it has been commonly linked with cerebral palsy. Toxoplasmosis is a less familiar infectious disease caused by a parasite that infects cats. The disease produces such mild symptoms that infected adults may be unaware that they have it, yet toxoplasmosis may cause cerebral palsy in a developing fetus.

Poisons in the mother's system also are passed on to the unborn child. Absorption during pregnancy of trace amounts of toxic materials such as lead, arsenic, and other heavy metals from paint or other sources can cause brain damage in the fetus. Maternal diseases such as diabetes and anemia may also increase the risk of health problems for the child.

Dr. Little made a useful observation when he connected premature birth with cerebral palsy. Roughly one out of every three cases of cerebral palsy involve prematurity or low birth weight. This factor has been especially linked with the spastic form of cerebral palsy.

Normal-sized, nine-month-pregnancy babies are supported by the mother's system until their systems are developed enough to operate independently. Premature babies may be cut off from the mother's placenta before they are fully developed. The result may be serious breathing and circulation problems that interfere with brain development.

Low birth weight may be an indication of poor

Low-birth weight babies (bottom) are three times as likely to have CP than normal-birth weight children.

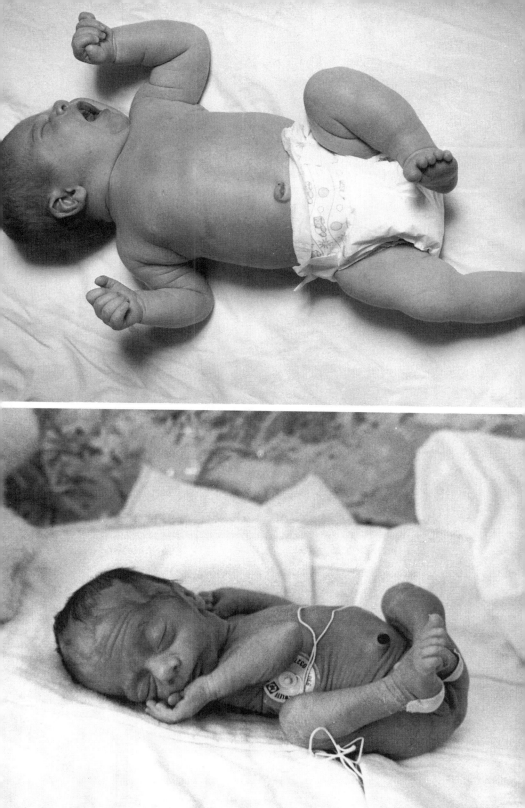

nutrition or health habits in the mother. The common expression that a pregnant mother is "eating for two" is accurate. A mother who does not ingest the proper nutrients, especially protein, may not necessarily suffer any serious short-term effects herself. But she will be unable to supply her vulnerable fetus with proper nutrients for growth, and brain damage can result.

The link between poor nutrition and birth problems can be traced back many years, even to the mother's childhood. Recent studies have shown that women who were undernourished in their growing years, or who ate mostly junk food—high-sugar, low-nutrition snacks and beverages—run an added risk of giving birth to a child with health problems.

Research has also documented the fact that women who smoke regularly have smaller babies and thereby increase the risk of cerebral palsy in their children. Pregnant women who smoke heavily or drink alcoholic beverages, or are subjected to X rays also increase the chances of having a brain-damaged child.

Brain Damage During Labor and Birth

It has been said that the short journey down the birth canal is the most dangerous trip that many people will ever take. After nine months in a protected environment, the baby is suddenly and rather violently pushed out into the world and cut off from his umbilical supply line. There is ample opportunity in this process for the two primary causes of brain damage— injury and lack of oxygen—to occur.

The normal contractions of the uterus, which are necessary for pushing the baby out, subject the baby to a large amount of pressure and stress. This stress may be severe enough to cut back the baby's circulation and cut off oxygen to the brain. The head is also

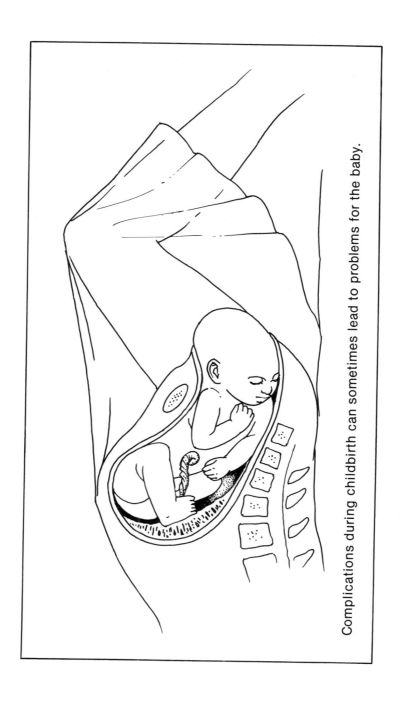

Complications during childbirth can sometimes lead to problems for the baby.

squeezed during birth. While the flexible skull of most babies is able to withstand this, an abnormal amount of pressure can create problems.

Given the amount of stress put upon a baby during delivery, anything that prolongs labor or complicates delivery puts the baby further at risk. Breech deliveries, in which the baby enters the birth canal rear end first, and difficult deliveries, in which the baby must be pulled out with forceps, increase the chances of cerebral palsy. Late pregnancies and deliveries can also cause circulation problems. First-born children were once thought to be more likely to acquire cerebral palsy at birth because delivery is usually most difficult with the first child, but this has not been supported by studies.

Another potential cause of cerebral palsy associated with birth is infection with Herpes Virus 2, a virus that causes herpes. Babies can contract the disease while in the birth canal of an infected mother. This produces some sort of brain damage in 5 to 10 percent of those babies infected.

Jaundice, which may occur in newborns, has also been linked with cerebral palsy. This condition, which shows up as a yellowing of the skin, is caused by a build-up of bile pigments in the bloodstream that can destroy brain cells.

Currently, experts believe that most cases of cerebral palsy are due to factors early in pregnancy rather than events occurring near the actual birth.

Brain Damage During Infancy

About 90 percent of cerebral palsy cases occur before or during birth. Cerebral palsy acquired in this way is known as *congenital* cerebral palsy. Cerebral palsy caused by factors that occur after birth is *acquired* cerebral palsy. This occurs most commonly as a result of head injuries from falls or hard blows to the head; infections such as encephalitis and meningitis, poisoning by lead, carbon monoxide, and other substances, and malnutrition. While seizures are often indicators of brain damage, repeated severe seizures early in infancy can also *cause* brain damage.

Medical research has uncovered only some of the situations or events that can lead to cerebral palsy. Every year, cases of cerebral palsy occur in normal-weight, full-term babies with normal deliveries and no apparent illness or injuries.

Preventing Cerebral Palsy

Since cerebral palsy cannot be cured, the only way to limit the number of cases is to prevent the brain damage that causes it. Obviously, given the great many possible causes of brain damage, there are no simple means of prevention. But medical research and new technologies have provided some ways to reduce the risk of this brain damage.

As noted earlier, the mother's nutrition and health habits have been found to play important roles in proper growth and brain development in the fetus. The simplest step that a mother can take toward preventing cerebral palsy, then, is to make certain she takes good care of herself. A well-balanced, nutritious diet is a good start. The U.S. government has programs available to provide food and nutrition counseling for those who need help.

In addition, pregnant women should avoid chemicals or poisons that can cause low-birth weight babies and harm their brain development. These chemicals include alcohol, tobacco, and any drug or medication that is not cleared by a physician. Avoiding cats or

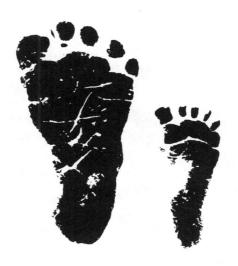

Guess which baby's mother did drugs while she was pregnant.

If you're pregnant, see a doctor now.
Fight low birthweight.
March of Dimes
Campaign For Healthier Babies

A March of Dimes ad warning about the effects of drugs on newborn children.

cat litter will reduce the chances of infection with toxoplasmosis.

The medical profession has made great strides in learning about the causes and prevention of cerebral palsy. Some of the dangers of fetal brain damage can be reduced if parents seek out medical care early in pregnancy, and follow the recommendations given. Medical professionals can monitor the health of the mother and alert her to deficiencies in diet and other factors that might result in low birth weight. Medical engineering advances have also allowed more artificial supports for very premature babies to keep them alive and healthy.

One of the more recent tools developed by medical researchers is the technique of amniocentesis. This involves taking a sample from the fluid that surrounds the baby in the amniotic sac and analyzing it in a laboratory. Although this technique cannot detect cerebral palsy, it can detect chemical imbalances and other signs that indicate a potential problem in getting oxygen to the brain.

Thanks to another recent medical advance, physicians are able to penetrate the mysteries of the human brain without cutting open the skull. Computerized tomography (CT) is a technique in which hundreds of X-ray pictures of the brain are taken from different angles. A computer then puts all this information together to reproduce a three-dimensional picture—a CT scan—of the brain. This makes it possible to detect bleeding and abnormal or damaged structures in the brain. Ultrasound technology is being developed that can easily detect blood clots or swelling of tissues in the brain. This technique sends high-frequency vibrations into the body and uses the echo from these vibrations to form rough images of the features within the body. Ultrasound can also give a clearer picture of the baby's development during pregnancy.

Vaccines have been developed for certain bacterial and viral infections that may cause cerebral palsy. The incidences of rubella, a frequent contributor to cerebral palsy prior to 1960, have been drastically reduced by immunization. Medical research has also begun to identify which infectious diseases carry a risk of cerebral palsy (herpes being one example). Common infectious diseases that may cause brain damage in the very young can be prevented by routine immunization. The risk of herpes infection during delivery can be removed by performing a Caesarean section, in which the baby is surgically removed through the uterus rather than allowed to travel into the birth canal.

The problem of blood disorders leading to cerebral palsy can easily be prevented. After each pregnancy, a mother with Rh blood incompatibility can be injected with a serum that prevents destructive antibodies from forming. Babies born with blood disorders can be given blood transfusions to reduce the problem. Treatment is also available to quickly clear up the dangerous condition of jaundice in the newborn.

Hospital labor and delivery rooms are now equipped with a variety of technological improvements that reduce the chances of brain damage during birth. Sensitive instruments that can detect small changes in the respiration of both the mother and the baby help alert physicians to potential problems. Oxygen masks assist the mother's and baby's respiration. Intravenous injections pump extra supplies of nutrients to mothers and babies who need it. Physicians rely less on drugs and medication for the mother during delivery to protect the baby from their effects, and greater care is exercised with the use of forceps in difficult deliveries.

All these advances have succeeded in reducing the numbers of children born with cerebral palsy. Figures from the United Cerebral Palsy Associations show that in recent decades the number of new cerebral palsy cases appears to have been cut in half.

That figure could be further reduced by education. Insights into the prevention of cerebral palsy are of no use if people are not aware of them or choose to ignore them. Although rubella is easily preventable, the National Institutes of Health has estimated that perhaps as much as 20 percent of the women now entering childbearing age run the risk of brain-damaged children because they have not been immunized. A renewed effort must be made to alert parents and others of ways to reduce the risk of cerebral palsy.

Further research and medical improvements could prevent even more cerebral palsy, particularly in those cases for which no cause can as yet be determined. Despite improvements in medical care, there has been no reduction in the percentage of underweight babies born in the United States. The precise causes of low birth weight, and the exact role of nutrition, have yet to be clearly identified. A great deal of research remains to be done concerning the chemical changes that take place in a damaged or undeveloped brain. Techniques used in amniocentesis and in brain scans can be improved to allow even greater supervision over potential problems in pregnancy and delivery.

The most difficult cases of all to prevent are those acquired by accident or injury after birth. While accidents are not totally preventable, there is room for improvement in our understanding of how such accidents occur and how they could be prevented.

3

Detecting Cerebral Palsy

As with any disease or disability, the sooner cerebral palsy is detected, the better it can be managed. Unfortunately, there has never been a test that doctors can perform to prove whether a child does or does not have cerebral palsy. No infectious bacteria is present, no pain, no noticeable swelling or fever or rash. Cerebral palsy strikes the brain, the most inaccessible part of the human body. The same solid skull that protects the brain from injury also prevents physicians from examining the brain to look for signs of injury.

For the most part, the only clues that cerebral palsy exists are in the damage that it does. Unfortunately, these clues begin to show up only after the damage has already been done. A serious problem with the heart or the lungs is more likely to attract immediate attention. Because normally at birth these organs are performing the tasks for which they were designed, a defect in either will likely affect the child's performance from the start and will therefore be detected.

Cerebral palsy, however, is a developmental condition that affects a system that grows and changes over the years. It is very rarely detected at birth. A normal newborn child has no more voluntary control over his or her muscles than a child with severe brain damage. The muscular movements that any newborn needs to perform in order to survive are governed strictly by reflex actions. Motions such as sucking, kicking, and crying occur automatically, with no conscious effort on the part of the child. Therefore a cerebral palsied newborn will act much the same as a normal newborn and may appear to be completely normal for several weeks, sometimes longer.

Only as the normal child begins to develop control over his or her muscles and relies less on reflexes does the story of cerebral palsy begin to unfold. Diagnosing cerebral palsy is primarily a matter of comparing a child's neuromuscular control with that of a normal child at that age. Large gaps between the two are viewed with suspicion.

In the past, some of the more subtle clues were not understood and cerebral palsy was not detected until the child had difficulty learning to walk. Now, most children, particularly those with the more common spastic cerebral palsy, are diagnosed well before their first birthday. Although athetoid cerebral palsy may take longer to confirm, few cases go undetected for more than a year or two. With any type of cerebral palsy, the more severe the condition, the sooner the disabilities will become apparent.

Some early indications of cerebral palsy have to do with the child's behavior. Infants who are listless, groggy, difficult to wake, or extremely passive bear close watching for further signs of cerebral palsy. To a lesser degree, extraordinary hyperactivity or irritability may be indicators of brain damage. Feeding problems are another early cerebral palsy indicator.

*Do you see any signs of CP in these children?
The child, at right, has "lazy eye," which may be
a symptom of CP, according to an expert who
studied this photograph. He said the other child
has no visible signs of the disease.*

Refusal to eat, unusually fussy behavior during eating, difficulty with sucking or swallowing, or inability to stay awake during eating are signs there may be trouble.

There may also be early physical indications such as exceptionally weak muscles or poor muscle response. An infant with cerebral palsy may have difficulty supporting its head at all when lifted. One of the earliest physical indicators is the infant's ability to raise its head while lying down. Most infants are able to do this by about three months of age; a child with cerebral palsy will be slower.

Seizures or convulsions are connected with disturbances of the brain and may be another indicator. While seizures are relatively rare among the general population, they occur in one-quarter to one-third of those with cerebral palsy.

As the child continues to grow, the gap in muscle control between those with and without cerebral palsy becomes more obvious. Children with cerebral palsy may have trouble with balance or with reaching, sitting, crawling, standing, or walking, or they may be late in developing these skills. Speech may be difficult or impossible. A youngster with cerebral palsy may display unusual or awkward muscle movements or posture or may use one side of his body more than the other.

By preschool age, the child will usually show the characteristic signs of cerebral palsy, such as holding one arm tightly against the body, and may walk with a lilting gait, bouncing on the toes. Even the mildest cases of cerebral palsy become apparent by first grade.

Problems in Diagnosing Cerebral Palsy

Even when these signs are exhibited, cerebral palsy may be difficult to distinguish from other childhood

This twelve-year-old boy has the same motor control
as a one-month-old baby. He cannot walk or talk,
and he can communicate only with eye movements
and other facial expressions.

disabilities. The same clues that point toward cerebral palsy may also be indicators of nutritional problems, physical disorders, bone deformities, allergies, psychological disorders, or even a brain tumor.

In addition, some of the disabilities that accompany cerebral palsy may overshadow the condition. For example, cerebral palsy does not cause mental retardation, but in some cases the brain damage that causes cerebral palsy also affects the person's mental capacity. Severe mental retardation can affect the behavior of the child in ways that make it hard to determine if cerebral palsy is also present. Obvious physical disabilities such as blindness and hearing loss may also distract attention away from cerebral palsy symptoms.

The reverse is also true. The effects of cerebral palsy may mask other problems or may cause doctors to misdiagnose related problems. For example, it is difficult to determine the intelligence level of a child who has such a severe case of cerebral palsy that he or she cannot communicate in the normal way. All too often in the past, such children were labeled as mentally retarded, when the problem may simply have been an inability to handle the materials used in learning, such as pencils and books. The problem is compounded by the fact that cerebral palsy may be accompanied by learning disabilities, for example, the inability to focus attention on one task for more than a few minutes.

A tragic example of the dangers of misdiagnosis is Ruth Sienkiewicz-Mercer. She acquired cerebral palsy at the age of five from an attack of encephalitis. Diagnosed as mentally retarded at the age of six, she spent most her remaining childhood years in state institutions. Her frequent efforts to communicate with facial expressions were dismissed as involuntary muscle contractions or mindless contortions. Not until an attendant at one of the institutions noticed that she laughed at some fairly subtle adult humor did anyone suspect she was not retarded. Ruth, who is now married and living independently, described her situation in a book, *I Raise My Eyes to Say Yes*, published in 1989. Her story illustrates the importance of distinguishing between physical barriers to learning, learning disabilities, and retardation.

Similarly, the grimacing and other unnatural facial expressions of athetoid cerebral palsy, which are nothing more than involuntary reflex actions of the facial muscles, may give the impression of emotional or mental problems.

Parents are often the first to notice some of the signs of cerebral palsy. Many means are available to help parents detect signs of the condition and to help them determine how severe the case. But the complex nature of cerebral palsy makes it essential that skilled professionals be brought in as quickly as possible. Proper diagnosing of cerebral palsy is a long, involved process that requires a great deal of skill.

Detecting the Hidden Effects of Cerebral Palsy

When we think of disabilities, especially ones involving the muscles, we tend to think of them as strictly physical problems. The person cannot walk or talk or pick up objects. In recent years, however, the medical profession has paid more attention to the fact that physical handicaps can produce emotional and psychological problems.

No typical psychological behavior or typical personality is common to persons with cerebral palsy. They show as wide a range in these areas as the general population. Yet a proper diagnosis of cerebral palsy must take any related problems into account. Some psychological and emotional problems may be related to the brain injury that produced the cerebral

47

palsy. If the areas of the brain that govern emotions and personality are damaged, the emotions and personality can be altered, causing hyperactivity, for example.

Emotional and psychological problems may also come about *because* of the disability. A normal small child, for example, may flinch and squirm when a parent washes his or her face, or fuss and stiffen when a parent dresses the child in a shirt the child does not like. A severely disabled child may have no defense at all, no way to communicate a protest, no way to fight against it. Continually being forced to submit to actions that he does not like, without any means of defense, can cause intense frustration. So can the inability to communicate thoughts or feelings, to share affection, to perform a simple task, to play active games with other children, or to move about freely.

Since no parent wants his or her child to be disabled in any way, the discovery that a child has cerebral palsy may cause negative feelings in the parents. When eight-month-old Rick Hoyt was diagnosed as having cerebral palsy, his father, Dick, found it difficult to develop normal feelings of affection for the boy. As Rick became fully grown, the two finally developed an unusual form of interaction. Dick and Rick began training together for triathlons.

This activity brought them national attention. In one race, Dick swam 2.4 miles while towing Rick in a rubber raft. He followed this by biking 112 miles with Rick in a special basket, and finished the contest by pushing his son 26.2 miles in a wheelchair. The shared effort of these grueling ordeals was able to tear down the barriers between them.

A parent's negative feelings can take the form of anger, or of depression, or of rejection of the child. If these feelings are not controlled, they may prevent normal parent–child bonding, or they may communicate to the child a feeling of being unloved. On the

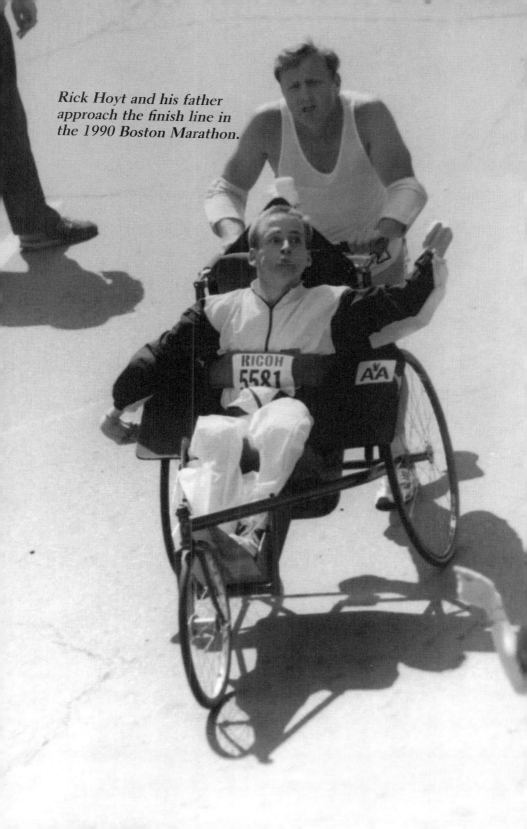

Rick Hoyt and his father approach the finish line in the 1990 Boston Marathon.

other hand, parents may feel so sorry for the child that they indulge in pampering and impose no discipline.

Persons with severe disabilities also experience the frustration of being dependent on others for many of their wants and needs. This can result in the feeling that they are inferior to others, or even that they are a burden to those who care for them. Such feelings may be reinforced when people tease them or make inconsiderate comments about them, or when others constantly avoid them or show discomfort around them. When the normal challenges of growing and developing are compounded by these difficulties, the development of a healthy and stable personality may be at risk.

For all these reasons, it is not enough simply to determine whether or not a child has cerebral palsy. A thorough evaluation of a child suspected of having cerebral palsy involves:

- a family history to determine if genetic or nutritional factors might be a cause of cerebral palsy.
- a physical examination by a medical professional to determine what muscles are affected and how severely they are disabled. These include the muscles involved in speech as well as those used in walking and performing tasks.
- laboratory work such as an electroencephalogram that can measure changes in the brain structures.
- tests to determine mental ability, possible learning disabilities, and the effects of the conditions on the child's mental and emotional well-being.

The results of these evaluations offer both family and professionals a much better understanding of the specific challenges that cerebral palsy brings to each individual.

4

Treating Cerebral Palsy

The description of cerebral palsy as an incurable condition may give the impression that little can be done about the condition once it develops. It is true that children with cerebral palsy will be challenged by muscle coordination difficulties all of their lives, and that there is little chance of dramatic improvement. For this reason, treatment programs were not even considered for many decades after cerebral palsy was first identified.

But while cerebral palsy cannot be cured or reversed, it can be *managed*. There are ways to help people learn to cope with many of the difficulties that arise, to help them overcome some of their physical limitations, and to help them adapt to their situation.

Cerebral palsy is such a complex, varied group of conditions that no simple treatments will help all cases. Programs have to be tailored to the person's situation, and this often requires a number of specialists working closely together with the parents. An accurate understanding of the child's full range of abilities and disabilities is extremely important to make sure that the child is given a program of treatment that is useful and safe.

Muscle Therapy

Three main types of exercises work to improve the muscle coordination of a person with cerebral palsy: physical therapy, occupational therapy, and speech/language therapy.

Physical therapy consists of exercises, activities, and games designed to improve the basic control of the muscles. The program is supervised by a professional physical therapist, and each activity is designed to help a specific muscular control problem. A person can accomplish little without the ability to keep the trunk and head somewhat steady, and physical therapy works on this first. Some exercises work to improve a person's balance; others loosen very rigid muscles and help make the person more flexible. Depending upon the skill level of the person, physical therapy can involve wheelchair operation, walking, climbing stairs, and activities involving the hands and fingers.

One type of physical therapy attempts to "reeducate" the affected muscles—help them to "unlearn" reflex actions so they are better able to perform controlled tasks. This is done by pushing against the reflex action. A typical exercise consists of forcing the muscle into a position or action opposite from what the reflex tries to do. For example, an arm that is constantly contracted close to the body may be pulled out away from the body.

While physical therapy works at improving general coordination and flexibility, occupational therapy concentrates on the basic skills that a person

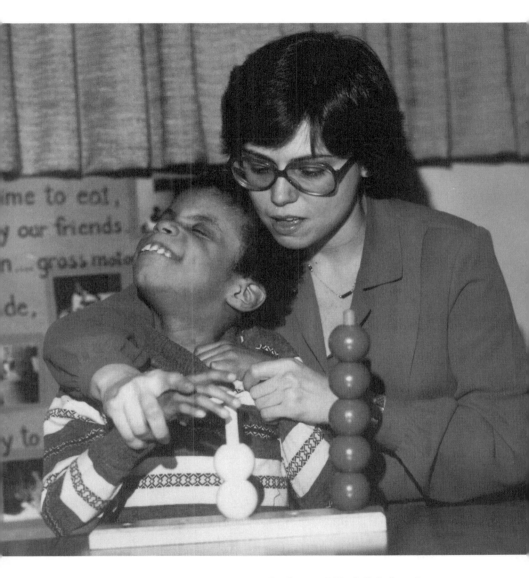

*An occupational therapist helps a CP child develop
better eye-hand coordination.*

needs to live independently. These tasks often include more eye–hand coordination and more delicate skills involving the fingers. For younger children and those with more severe cerebral palsy, the tasks may include such things as dressing, holding a cup or a spoon, and learning to use the toilet. Some children may need help in learning to chew or swallow. An older child might learn how to hold a pencil or how to work a computer. Occupational therapy teaches such adult skills as cooking and cleaning and may include job training.

Speech/communication therapy is for those who lack normal control over the muscles used in speech and for those with hearing problems.

Exercises in any of the above areas of therapy can be difficult and repetitive. There is a limit as to how much muscular control a person with cerebral palsy can gain, and the progress may seem slow. But all these types of therapy help the exerciser gain some independence and confidence by allowing him or her to perform new tasks, to perform old tasks more easily, or to communicate more easily, or by simply preventing the current disabilities from getting worse.

Specialized Equipment

Many mechanical aids are available to provide some freedom of motion to persons who have limited use of muscles. Braces may be used to support weak muscles and to help set the muscles in a more useful position. Wheelchairs, either manually operated or electric, are commonly used to help those who cannot walk or who walk only with great difficulty.

Typewriters and computers are important tools for those who lack the hand coordination to write with a pencil. The tremendous growth of microcomputer technology has proven a great blessing to those with cerebral palsy. Computers have helped produce more

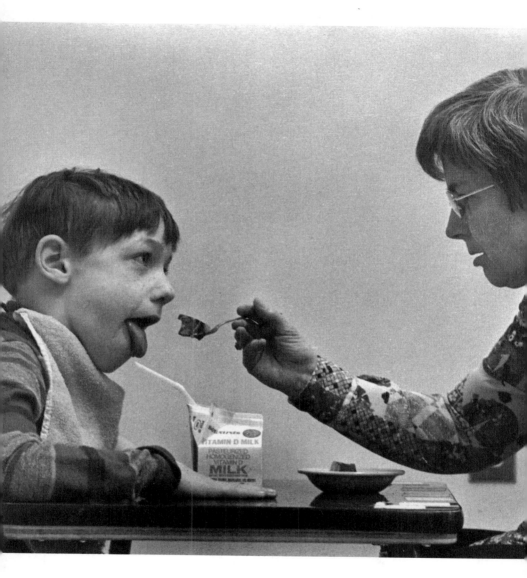

For most people, eating is
a pleasurable activity but for this
CP child, it is a skill to
be learned and practiced.

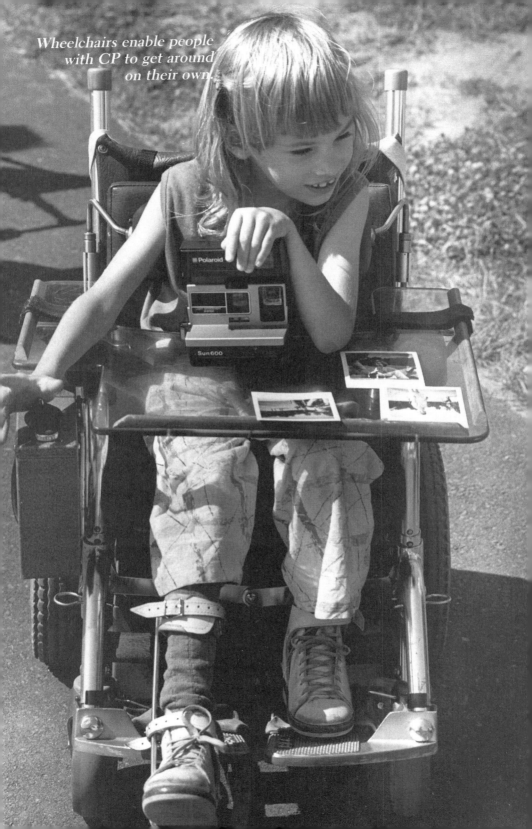

Wheelchairs enable people with CP to get around on their own.

*A special keyboard is handy for people
with CP who are unable to work with
a regular computer keyboard.*

jobs that require working with numbers and information (which do not require great muscle control) rather than handling objects (which does require control).

Many ingenious devices are continually being engineered to help those with limited muscle control participate more fully in activities. For example, keyguards can be placed over a computer keyboard so that a person without normal finger control can slide a hand along the guard toward the proper key without accidentally bumping other keys. Those with virtually no hand control can use "unicorns"—sticks attached to a band wrapped around the head—to jab at keys.

Push-button electronic control has placed a great many tasks within the grasp of disabled persons. Automatic door openers, automatic can openers, and scoopers that help get food to their mouths are just a few of the many devices available.

The danger in using specialized equipment of this sort is that it can provide a ready crutch where none is needed. Persons who with some effort might be able to develop better muscle control cannot improve if they begin to rely heavily on such devices too early in life. While it might be easier for a child to move around with a wheelchair, early and continuous use of a wheelchair may prevent the child from learning to walk.

Surgery and Medication

Currently few types of surgery are of much use in treating cerebral palsy. The damage to the brain has been done and cannot be repaired. While some operations could improve muscle control, physicians generally recommend physical therapy for this. Surgery can be used in some cases, however, to prevent or correct deformities. A surgical procedure is often

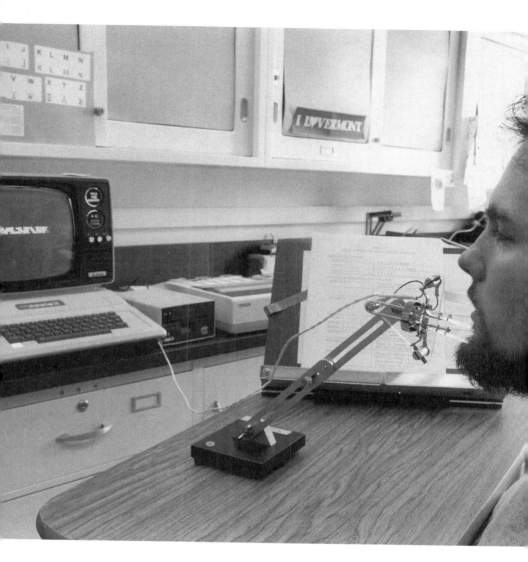

*A chin switch can be used
to operate a computer
by people unable to
use their hands.*

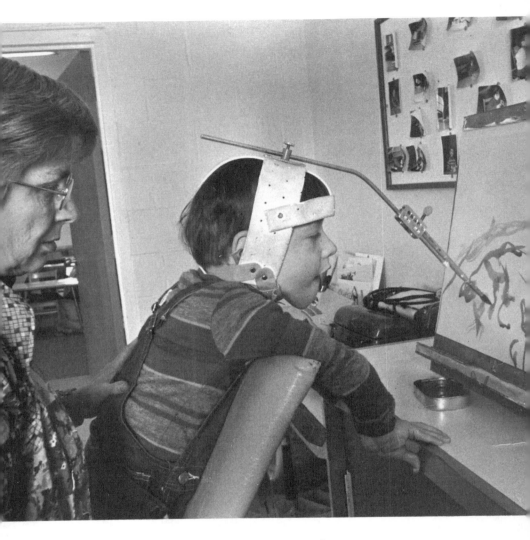

A "unicorn" is another
useful device when
the hands can't
do the job.

used on children with tightly contracted leg muscles that force the child to walk on his or her toes. An operation on the heel tendons can sometimes release this contraction and make it easier to walk. Even this, however, is no substitute for muscle exercises but is simply a way to make physical therapy more effective.

Medication can do little to help an incurable condition. Some of the extreme tension in the muscles that is common with cerebral palsy, however, can be eased with muscle-relaxant drugs. Medication can also be used to control some of the related disabilities, especially seizures and convulsions. Behavior problems such as moodiness and hyperactivity, and learning disabilities such as attention deficit disorder, may respond to a carefully supervised program of medication.

Psychotherapy

Although the physical disabilities may be the most obvious concern in treating someone with cerebral palsy, they may not be the most important. A slight improvement in muscle control will mean little if the person is devastated by emotional and personality problems. Younger children are often unaware that something is wrong with them. But by the elementary-school years, they often become very conscious of being different and realize that this problem is not going to go away. The teenage years are often difficult years as young people try to find ways to fit into the world. Disabled teenagers have the same needs as any other teenager, but their problems of adjustment may be multiplied. Some sort of counseling may be needed to help improve self-confidence, help the person deal with frustration and emotional problems, and improve his or her ability to deal with social situations.

Experimental Treatments

Advances in cerebral palsy treatment have been hampered by the fact that so few cases are exactly alike. Nevertheless, some promising areas of treatment are now being explored.

One of these is called *biofeedback*, a form of physical therapy designed to relax the reflex tension that prevents the muscles from being used properly. It is often difficult for people to concentrate on exercising or controlling a particular muscle or set of muscles. Biofeedback attacks this problem by translating the degree of tension in a muscle into a simple visual or audio signal on an electronic device. As the muscle is contracted more tightly, the device produces a higher or louder musical tone. As it relaxes, the device may produce a lower or quieter note. In this way the exerciser instantly knows whether his or her actions are achieving the desired results. Although no one knows exactly why this technique works, biofeedback has been successful in bringing about some improvement in muscle control. Further studies may help professionals make even greater use of this technique.

The knowledge that nerves can be stimulated by electrical impulses has led some researchers to look into experimental brain surgery. It may be possible to implant electrodes in the brain that would trigger activity in nerves that have been damaged by cerebral palsy. A similar technique, which would not require surgery, would involve electrodes attached to the affected limbs.

Biochemistry is another area of hope in the fight against cerebral palsy. Scientists are beginning to learn more about the chemical makeup of the nervous system. Nerve cells are known to give off minute bursts of energy and when they do so, they release minute amounts of chemicals called neuro-transmitters, which control communication among nerve cells. Chemical activity is also involved in the growth and maintenance of the nervous system. Scientists are trying to figure out what is happening in these chemical reactions. Once the process is understood, they may be able to discover how brain damage disrupts this process. Perhaps drug treatments can be developed that would restore the chemical balance needed for proper muscle control.

A technique of brain scanning called positive emission transverse tomography (PETT) may provide physicians with a powerful tool for seeing into the brain. Rather than taking a still "photograph" as current brain scans do, PETT is being refined so that it will observe a "moving picture" of the brain. This technique traces a radioactive form of a nutrient as it goes to the brain by measuring the bursts of energy produced by the nutrient. The greater the energy measured at a particular point, the greater the activity of the brain cells at that point. This may enable researchers to pinpoint which portions of the brain direct specific actions or specific muscles. If scientists can discover the difference in brain activity between a normal child and one with cerebral palsy, they may begin to understand how to correct the problem.

Parental Involvement in Treatment Programs

Cerebral palsy treatment has little chance of succeeding unless the parents are informed and actively involved in the treatment. A strong relationship between parent and child is most effective in giving the child the support and encouragement needed to deal with challenges. Parents are in a position to know best

*As is true of all kids, those with CP need
lots of attention from their parents.*

the child's frustrations and problems. Since they have the most contact with the child, they have many opportunities to help the child work on physical and occupational therapy skills.

On the other hand, it is all too easy for parents to fall into behaviors that create barriers to growth. Professional assistance can help them to recognize and eliminate harmful behavior. Some parents may have trouble accepting their disabled child. Some may be under emotional or physical stress from caring for the extra needs of the child. They may have trouble coping with situations in which their child is teased, or stared at, or pitied. They may be overcome with sudden feelings of anger or grief at the thought of what their child may have to miss as he or she grows up. While some parents are able to deal with these situations without outside assistance, others may benefit from professional counseling.

Even parents who love and cherish their child may express such disappointment over their child's handicaps that the child feels unwanted. Parents may feel so sorry for the child that they do not enforce the discipline that any child needs in order to learn proper behavior. Parents may think that cerebral palsy prevents their child from performing certain tasks or acting in certain ways, when the child is quite capable of doing so. Parents may insist that the child live under their care all through life even though he or she is perfectly capable of living independently. Close parental involvement in the treatment program and in parent support groups can eliminate some of these problems.

5

Travis and Adam: Growing Up with Cerebral Palsy

What does it feel like to have cerebral palsy? In a condition that can take so many different forms, there can be no one answer to that question. One could no more describe a typical day in the life of a person with cerebral palsy than one could describe a typical day in the life of an American.

But you can at least get a feel for what it is like to grow up with the condition by hearing the stories of Travis and Adam, two boys who face greatly different challenges in growing up with cerebral palsy.

It's All in the Smile

At first glance, the room seems to be a magical playground. Stuffed with bright colors, balls of all shapes and sizes, motorized vehicles, and curious contraptions, it attracts children like a huge magnet. It is a physical therapy room, and right now it has a single, important purpose for seven-year-old Travis: It is there to help him learn how to hold his head steady.

Travis was born two months premature and

struggled with serious respiratory problems during his first weeks of life. The cerebral palsy that resulted left him with so little control over his muscles that he cannot run, walk, stand, or even sit by himself on the floor. He is also severely affected by other disabilities. His vision is very limited. Although he can make sounds, he cannot speak. He has virtually no way of communicating except with his warm smile. He is mentally retarded, although his inability to communicate makes it difficult to determine how much he is capable of understanding.

Travis lives with his mother and an older brother. Despite all his cerebral palsy challenges, he attends the same elementary school as his normal older brother. The two do not travel to school together, however. Travis arrives in a special bus that has room for his wheelchair. As he sits in his wheelchair, a wide door in the middle of the bus opens, and an electrically operated elevator lowers the chair to the ground.

Travis's class has more teachers than the average classroom. Today there are seven other special-needs children in class, and four adults to help them learn. A special treat awaits Travis this morning: an all-school program in the gymnasium put on by a clown who is there to promote reading. Although Travis cannot read, and can see little of the action, he enjoys being part of the group.

Travis's wheelchair is ideal for supporting and transporting him, but it is not good for him to be in it all day. He needs to move around to a variety of positions. Back in his classroom, he is put in a bolster chair. His stiff legs are placed on either side of a chair that looks like a small, padded balance beam with a back on it. Straps help to hold him up, and a desk is slid in front of him. Travis's head control is often best when he is in this chair, and he smiles at the praise from his teachers.

A short time later, Travis is moved to the prone

stander, a padded board tilted at an angle against a high table. Although he is small, he is so stiff that two adults are needed to lift him onto the stander, to place his feet in the wooden supports, and to get his legs straight rather than turned toward each other. This is as close as Travis can come to standing—lying at an angle, as if on a steep sliding board with his chin over the top edge. Again he is strapped in for support. His arms are free to move across the desk and they wave around in no particular pattern, his fingers and hands curled inward.

Today the class is making apple prints. They take an apple that is cut in half, dip it into paint, and stamp the image on a sheet of paper. Travis's hands are too stiff for him to pick up the apple. A teacher dips it into the paint for him, puts it on the paper, takes his hand, and helps him press down on it. Soon the page is filled with bright red designs.

Then a plastic sailor toy is anchored to his table by suction. For a while Travis rolls his head back to look up at the lights—he is able to see something there that fascinates him. He notices the toy after he bumps it with his hand. He begins to bat at it with his left hand—his better hand, the one he uses for support when he lies on the floor.

Even though he is unable to grasp anything with his hands, he can operate a touch radio. This toy has two huge round buttons on either side. Travis does not have to push the buttons. If he so much as touches the left button, the radio gives off a buzzing alarm noise. The right-hand one plays music. Travis can get both to work and seems to prefer the music to the alarm.

It's time for another shift in positions. Travis is carried back to the bolster chair for music time. Although this is a group activity, Travis cannot directly participate in groups. All of his learning must be done one-on-one with the teacher. While a couple of the other children are singing along, a teacher helps Travis join in by taking his arms and doing a little dance with them while she sings to him.

After his diapers are changed, it is time for lunch—one of the most important activities of the day. The lunchroom looks like a real kitchen and dining room, complete with round tables, sofas, sink, microwave, and refrigerator. With one adult for every one or two children, great attention is paid to helping the children to do as much for themselves as possible. Travis, of course, cannot hold a spoon or cup and so he cannot feed himself. But he still must do his part to make the meal a success: He must hold his head up in order to be fed. His teacher reminds him of this and waits for him to bring his head up against his headrest before feeding him a bite of stew.

The teacher feeds him small bits of bread, then encourages him to bite off a piece for himself. Travis likes the stew meat, but like many children he does not seem to be fond of vegetables. That is something he has no trouble communicating. He closes his mouth when he detects a pea or carrot on the spoon.

When lunch is finished, Travis is wheeled outside with his class for recess. They are the first ones out on this beautiful fall day. Unfortunately the warm weather and no breeze means the gnats are out. Travis and his classmates are unable to ward off the pesky insects as easily as others might. He sits beneath a shade tree and watches as the other children come out to play on swings. Occasionally he is taken for a stroll. Soon, however, he will be able to join in on the playground fun. A new playground is being completed on the school grounds, one that is specially designed for all children to play at together. The equipment may include a swinging platform that will enable him to swing while in his wheelchair.

Not every day is the same for Travis. Some days

he goes on a field trip to the "apartment." This is an actual apartment that the children use for occupational therapy. Some of them learn how to clean the room, find their way around, and maybe even make some lunch. Travis is limited in what he can do here.

Some days he goes to physical therapy or physical education. Since Travis has so little control over his head, he cannot use much of the equipment, such as the stair ramp, the four-sided ladder, the treadmill, or the rocker board. His teachers must spend their time trying to get him to relax his tense muscles. Sometimes the main goal of the class is to get him to stay relaxed for five to ten seconds.

Another goal is to strengthen his head support. His teacher tries to get him into a four-point stance with his knees and his hands, supported by a ball under his stomach. Someone else stands above him to entertain him so that he will lift his head to watch. Teachers also use this entertainment technique to help him to start tracking things with his eyes, in the hopes they will begin to focus better. Travis is also put stomach-down into a hammocklike swing and swung from side to side or back and forth as an exercise in learning to control his body. While he has too little control to learn to operate an electric wheelchair or to peddle a trike, he can move about some in a special electric trike operated by a lever that he pushes back and forth.

Since Travis's mother must work full time to support the family, a babysitter cares for Travis when he returns home after school. Many of the same toys and pieces of equipment at school (prone stander, bolster chair, electric switch toys) are available to him at home. He also enjoys lying on the floor and listening to his brother play Nintendo electronic games. Travis and his brother share a bedroom and get along better than most brothers!

Technology and education can do only so much for a person as severely affected by cerebral palsy as Travis. It is unlikely that he will ever dress himself, or use the bathroom himself, or feed himself. A couple of decades ago, society had little to offer persons such as Travis. Now at least he has the chance to build on the abilities that he does have. One day perhaps he will be able to grasp something in his hand. Perhaps he will continue to find his own ways of communicating.

For now, the clues as to what is going on in his mind must be read from his smile. Somehow, using only that smile, Travis can communicate more warmth than virtually any kid his age.

A Pretty Normal Life

Adam, a sixteen-year-old high school sophomore, lives out in the country a few miles from Travis. He, too, has cerebral palsy, but it is a less severe form. He has normal control over his arms and has no trouble with speech. Adam does not need a wheelchair for transportation since he can move around quite well with crutches. When he is at home and just moving about the house, he often walks without crutches.

Even though he has a twin brother and two sisters, Adam has a room of his own, and he is responsible for keeping it in order. He is an early riser—up by 6 AM—and he either rides the bus to school or else gets a ride from his brother.

The high school is a large, sprawling two-story building, and Adam uses the elevator when going up or down a floor. Other than that, his day is similar to that of most high school students. First period is English, not one of his favorites. But once he gets past an hour of studying verbs and sentence formation, he moves on to his favorite subject: cooking.

Adam has been taking cooking classes for a number of years. He has enjoyed making so many recipes that he does not have a specialty, although he has a soft spot in his heart for cookies. Today the class is making another favorite: pizza. Adam's dream is to own and operate a restaurant one day. In addition to polishing his cooking techniques, he plans to take some basic business courses and work some jobs in order to get the money to start his own business.

Third period is science, where the class is looking into microscopes at bacteria, some of the smaller inhabitants of our world. Adam has some learning disabilities, so even in a very large high school many of his classes are small so that he can receive individual attention. Only two other students are in his fourth-period math class. Each of them is allowed to work on problems at his own pace.

Following math and fifth-period social studies, Adam heads to the lunch room to eat with a group of his friends. He has no trouble making friends and does not restrict himself to just one best friend. "I consider all my friends to be good friends," he says.

Following the lunch break, he heads to the gym. Physical education is the main source of physical therapy for Adam. He takes part in a specially designed program that allows him to participate in regular sports activities such as volleyball.

During his final period of the day, Adam has a study hall, where he tries to get as much of his homework done as possible. Like other students, he enjoys extracurricular activities. Tonight is the big football game between his school and its closest rival. Adam will be there cheering his team on, as he does at most home games. He has also just joined the school newspaper staff and looks forward to cranking out articles.

When he returns home, Adam spends his time finishing homework, watching television, and doing chores. He helps with the dishes and sometimes runs the log splitter so the family can have enough wood for the cold winter nights. Adam's main hobby is collecting. His collections include baseball cards, comic books, and unusual key chains. He is particularly proud of his key chain collection, which he has gathered from all around the country and which includes "the smallest knife and the smallest lighter in the world."

Naturally, there are times when Adam misses being able to do some of the things that his friends and his brother and sisters are able to do. He would especially like to be able to ride a bike and to walk without crutches. But for the most part, his cerebral palsy does not dominate his life as it does someone like Travis. "It doesn't really bother me too much," says Adam. "You learn to live with it. Basically, I lead a pretty normal life."

6

Triumphing Over Cerebral Palsy

The challenges presented by cerebral palsy may be difficult, but they may be overcome. Many adults have learned to cope with their disabilities. Some of them have done so publicly; others have triumphed quietly on their own, far from the celebrity spotlight. Their stories are proof that conditions such as cerebral palsy cannot harm the human spirit.

Christy Brown—
Mr. "Left Foot"

Daniel Day-Lewis won the 1989 Academy Award for best actor for his portrayal of a remarkable Irishman in the motion picture *My Left Foot*. The subject of that film was Christy Brown, a man severely affected by cerebral palsy.

Brown was a "blue baby" (so-called because of the skin color caused by lack of oxygen during birth), born in 1933 just outside Dublin, Ireland. He had so little control over his muscles that he could not learn to crawl. He could not even sit up by himself.

At that time, little was known about cerebral

palsy. Brown, who had no control over facial expressions and the twisting, writhing movements of his hands, was diagnosed as mentally retarded. Since he was unable to talk or even to nod his head or raise an eyebrow, Brown could not demonstrate that he actually had a very active mind.

He was fortunate, however, in having a mother who was determined to include him in the Brown family life. She patiently read to him, carried him about, hugged him, attended to his needs, and talked to him constantly. One day when Brown was five, he was lying on the floor watching his sister write her school lesson on a slate. Desperate to find a way to unloose the thoughts sealed up inside his head, he jabbed his left foot toward the chalk.

Brown had made little use of that foot before, but he found that he had just a hint of control over those muscles, enough to help him break through. With much effort he clutched a piece of chalk with the foot and struggled to draw something. When his mother figured out that he was trying to draw the letter "A," Brown's shell of silence was broken. With encouragement from his mother and the rest of his large family, Brown learned to print the alphabet within the year. He then learned to produce enough sounds to make himself understood. His family refused to pamper him. His brothers carted him around in a modified wheelbarrow, and he even played goalie during their street soccer games.

One Christmas, Brown was fascinated by the paintbrush set that a brother had received as a present. He arranged a trade with the brother, and was soon working at producing accurate brush strokes, holding the brush with his left foot. He worked so hard at this that at the age of twelve, he entered one of his paintings in a contest for twelve- to sixteen-year-olds and won first prize!

In 1951, Dr. Robert Collis invited the eighteen-year-old Brown to his cerebral palsy clinic, the first of its kind in Ireland. As Brown was already fully grown, the intensive therapy program was not able to develop much muscle control beyond the incredible adaptations he had made with his left foot. He was, however, able to make some improvement in his speech.

Although he received wide acclaim as a painter, Brown turned to a different form of creativity: writing. Dr. Collis helped him write his autobiography, entitled *My Left Foot*, which was published in 1954. At the age of twenty-two, Christy Brown had achieved fame both as a painter and a writer. He later married and lived with his wife until his death at the age of forty-nine.

Christopher Nolan—
Secret Poet

Much of Christopher Nolan's life has followed the same path traveled by Christy Brown, so a comparison of their stories gives an idea of how the world is changing for those with cerebral palsy. Like Brown, Nolan is a Dublin Irishman, born twenty-two years later, in 1965. His disabilities, also caused by lack of oxygen to the brain during a difficult birth, have been even more severe than Brown's. Nolan was born with no use of his limbs, no speech, and virtually no control over the muscles of his neck.

Nolan's mother, however, recognized that her son had an unusual wit and intelligence. He was able to develop a creative method of communication by simply looking at different objects. By putting together the sequence of objects he looked at, his family was often able to figure out what he was trying to say. Nolan attended school at the Central Remedial Clinic in Dublin, beginning at the age of seven. Despite Christopher's inability to communicate, a psychologist was able to determine that his intelligence was well above average for his age.

What none of the Nolans knew, however, was that Christopher was writing poetry in his mind. Beginning at the age of three, he had spent long hours composing his verses and memorizing them, and he had prayed that someday he might be able to share them with others. That was finally made possible when he was eleven, with the help of medication and technology. The drug Lioresal was able to relax his neck muscles enough so that he could control the movements of his head for short periods of time. This allowed him to use a "unicorn" stick on his forehead to tap the keys of a typewriter. The Nolans bought him an electric typewriter and helped him type a thank-you letter. It was a slow process. Even with the medication, his mother still had to support his head while he typed. With his mother directing him to the right keys, it took ten or fifteen minutes of intense concentration for him to tap out each word.

But he soon surprised his mother by reaching for his own choice of letters. Not only could he spell, but he could write extraordinarily rich poetry with an enormous and sophisticated vocabulary. The attention he gained in winning a poetry award at the age of fourteen led to a gift of a microcomputer which helped him to increase his output to about four words per minute. At the age of sixteen he published a book of poetry, *Dam-Burst of Dreams*. Although unable to use his arms or legs in any way, Christopher Nolan had made his mark as one of Great Britain's most distinguished poets.

"Ten Thousand Things to Know"

"There are ten thousand things to know about a disabled person," says Mary, a professional guidance counselor. "One of those things is that he or she is disabled. If you leave it at that and do not get to know the person, you will not get to see the other nine thousand nine hundred and ninety-nine."

One of the first things you notice about Mary is that she has cerebral palsy. Hers is primarily an athetoid form of the condition. Many of her muscles contract and move in ways that she cannot control. She uses a wheelchair to get around, and although her speech is quite understandable, she must work very hard to make it so. If you go by first impressions, it might be easy to associate Mary strictly with cerebral palsy. But as you get to know her, you discover she is right. There are ten thousand things to know about her, and the more of those that you discover, the less you notice her cerebral palsy.

Mary developed cerebral palsy during birth, the most common source of the condition several decades ago. In her case, complications in delivery were so severe that her mother died during childbirth. Mary was diagnosed as having cerebral palsy in the first year of her life and was primarily raised by her grandmother. There was plenty of support from all members of her family, including eight brothers and sisters.

She credits this family support as the main reason for her success. "You have to have some network—family, friends, or other significant people in your life who believe in you, and who are there to bridge the bad times." Those persons she knows who must deal with cerebral palsy without such a network have a very hard time.

Mary is also thankful that she was not coddled as a youngster. The expectations put upon her during childhood set the tone for her entire life. She was expected to discover what her abilities were and to set her own pace based on those abilities, to "paddle my own canoe," as she puts it. The simple desire to keep up with so many older brothers and sisters provided a strong incentive for her to be as active as possible.

From kindergarten through second grade, Mary attended a special school for children with physical handicaps. But she was allowed to attend a regular public school following second grade. Many people her age who hear that are surprised, since the standard practice at the time was to keep special-needs children separated from the rest of society. Currently, the trend is toward mainstreaming, allowing children with special needs to work in a normal classroom as much as possible. Mary's school system was well ahead of its time. She stayed in the regular classroom and received physical and speech therapy right at school. "It was wonderful. I got to experience all the good stuff," she says.

Once she graduated from high school, however, the good stuff was harder to find. For most high school graduates, the choice is to go on to college, or get a job, or get married. For a disabled person, Mary says, "the choices are not that simple." Mary went on to college, but in order to do so, she had to continually prove herself. She had to take batteries of tests before getting into college. Unlike most freshmen, who are often feeling their way into a career, she was expected to explain exactly what her goals were in attending school in order to justify the extra expense of providing for her needs.

Mary graduated from college with a degree in English and then had to face an even harder lesson about what paths were available to a person with disabilities. There were few outside resources for her to turn to in seeking a job. She was on her own in trying to find a good working environment. Employers were leery of hiring a person with her disabilities. People who knew her were aware of what she could accomplish, and they would hire her for short-term jobs; those who did not know her would not hire her. Eventually, she returned to school. Her goal in earning a master's degree was to gain the knowledge and credentials necessary to provide families with some of the help that was unavailable to her.

She now works with a large number of children with cerebral palsy. "They are often taken aback when they meet me," she says. "They don't see themselves as adults having the same problems. The feeling is that if they do all their exercises, somehow it will get better. They meet me and say, 'Wait a minute! She's still like me. Why should I try?' The answer is that you need to work with the muscles you have." According to Mary, the whole point of physical therapy is to find different and creative ways to do the things that you want to do. Mary is glad that the trend is away from putting disabled people in safe, protected homes but instead encouraging them to be as independent as possible.

"I do almost all the things that other people do, only I do it differently," she says. She believes it is important for her to have "a place I can call my very own." Mary shares ownership of a house with an aunt and lives a very independent life. She enjoys fishing and swimming, although she is now so involved in her work that she has little time for either. She cannot drive a car but has found alternate ways to get where she needs to go. A special transit bus takes her to and from work. When her job requires her to travel in her ten-county territory, she may hire a driver. For shorter trips, she calls a taxi. Her disability does not prevent her from moving quickly around her office, often on a movable swivel chair. In fact, when she speaks of physical abilities that she would like to be able to improve, walking is far down on the list.

"If I could improve two things about myself, the first would be speaking," she says. For most people, tension makes speaking harder. "Multiply that tension ten times," she says and you get an idea of what it is like for her. She has done as well as she has in overcoming speech difficulties because "my career dictated that I had to be able to talk."

Her second wish is for better hand control: "So much would be easier if I had better hand control—writing, eating, picking up a phone." Despite lacking normal movement of the hands, she can grab a book off a shelf or pick up a thin brochure without much problem. It is all a result of a sometimes tedious trial-and-error process of finding a different way of doing things.

With her cheerful, outgoing nature, Mary has never had trouble making friends. Yet she still experiences the wall that people sometimes put up to keep themselves separate from those who are different. Occasionally when she is with a friend, other people will ask questions of her friend about Mary, as if she were not there or were not capable of answering for herself. She is aware that others sometimes avoid her.

Although this bothers her, she is able to sympathize with such people: "I think many of them are sensitive people who are afraid of offending. They back up and say, 'I don't know how to deal with this.' Some of them say they don't know whether a disabled person needs help in a particular situation. Why not ask them? They will tell you. If people can cross over this hump, they're all right."

Mary puts some of the responsibility for breaking down barriers on the disabled. "With a person in a wheelchair," she says, "it is hard for people to focus on the person separate from the hardware. It is up to the individual in the chair to project something."

She also sees problems stemming from the fact that children with cerebral palsy are on the receiving end of a great deal of help, so much so that they never experience the *other* person's need: "It is easy for kids to receive twenty-four hours a day. They need to learn how to give it back. Even if it is just a smile or a hug.

"My closest friends sometimes say, 'I forgot that you have cerebral palsy.' To me, that is the highest compliment.

"Cerebral palsy affects only the muscles, not the heart or soul."

EPILOGUE:
Cerebral Palsy
and Society

The actual cerebral palsy condition can be improved only slightly, over a long period of time. There is, however, great room for improvement in the attitudes of society toward people with cerebral palsy.

There will probably always be children, or even adults, who tease or mimic the disabled, or who stare at them, or who avoid having to be with them. These attitudes can be reduced, however, by educating people about cerebral palsy and other disabilities. The more people know about cerebral palsy, the more comfortable they are likely to be around those affected by this condition, and the more sensitive they will be to the person's feelings. Education will also help people to use terms that respect the dignity of the disabled and to avoid such demeaning words as "cripple," "poor, unfortunate," "wheelchairbound," and "victim."

Disabled persons have often had to rely on the charity of others simply because they are not given an opportunity to find useful work. In 1973, the federal

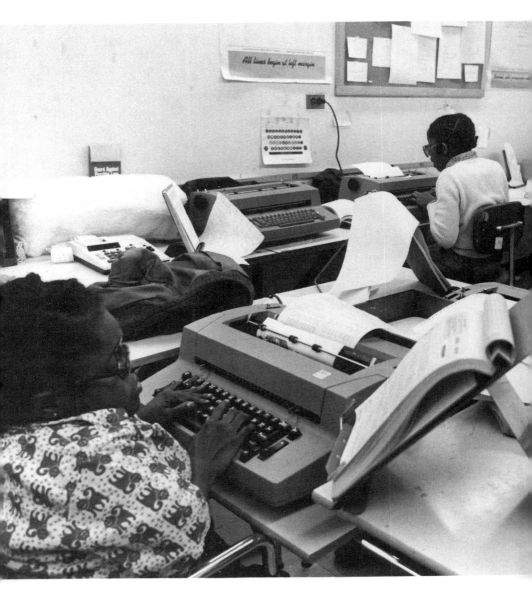

Youngsters with CP learning to type.

Kids with CP can succeed at tasks.

government took steps to eliminate this problem by passing a law requiring employers under federal contract to take active steps to insure that handicapped persons were hired and promoted within the ranks. Federal law also makes it illegal for anyone to discriminate against handicapped persons. Despite these steps, relatively few of the 200,000 working-age adults with cerebral palsy in the United States are employed.

Finally, public support is needed in order to finance research into the causes, prevention, and treatment of cerebral palsy. The United Cerebral Palsy Associations, the National Easter Seal Society, and the National Institutes of Health have been especially active in raising public awareness of cerebral palsy and in pleading the case for further cerebral palsy research.

For Information and Further Reading

Organizations

National Institutes of Health
Bethesda, MD 20205

The National Easter Seal Society, Inc.
2023 West Ogden Avenue
Chicago, IL 60612

United Cerebral Palsy Associations, Inc.
66 East 34th Street
New York, NY 10016

Books

Nonfiction

Brown, Christy. *My Left Foot*. London: Mandarin Paperbacks, 1989.

Kastner, Janet. *More Than the Average Guy: The Story of Larry Patton*. Canton, Ohio: Daring Books, 1989.

National Institutes of Health. *Cerebral Palsy: Hope Through Research*. Bethesda, Md.: 1980.

Nolan, Christopher. *Dam-Burst of Dreams*. Athens, Ohio: Ohio University Press, 1988.

———. *Under the Eye of the Clock: The Life Story of Christopher Nolan*. New York: St. Martin's Press, 1988.

Sienkiewicz-Mercer, Ruth, and Steven B. Kaplan. *I Raise My Eyes to Say Yes*. Boston: Houghton Mifflin, 1989.

Fiction

Aiello, Barbara, and Jeffrey Shulman. *It's Your Turn at Bat*. Frederick, Md.: Twenty-First Century Books, 1988.

Adler, C.S. *Eddie's Blue Winged Dragon*. New York: Putnam, 1988.

Gould, Marilyn. *Golden Daffodils*. Reading, Mass.: Addison-Wesley, 1982.

Little, Jean. *Mine For Keeps*. New York: Pocket Books, 1962.

Howard, Ellen. *Circle of Giving*. New York: Atheneum, 1984.

Slepian, Jan. *Alfred Summer*. New York: Macmillan, 1980.

———. *Lester's Turn*. New York: Macmillan, 1981.

Southhall, Ivan. *Let the Balloon Go*. New York: St. Martin's Press, 1968.

Index

93

94

About the Author

Nathan Aaseng has written nearly a hundred books for children, including titles on sports, nature, and science. He lives with his family in Wisconsin.